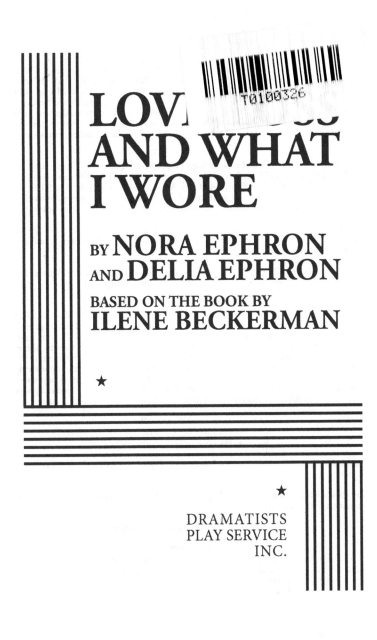

LOV[...] AND WHAT I WORE

BY NORA EPHRON AND DELIA EPHRON

BASED ON THE BOOK BY ILENE BECKERMAN

★

★

DRAMATISTS
PLAY SERVICE
INC.

LOVE, LOSS AND WHAT I WORE
Copyright © 2008, Nora Ephron and Delia Ephron

All Rights Reserved

NOTE ON BILLING

SPECIAL NOTE ON IMAGES

ACKNOWLEDGMENTS

THE AUTHORS WISH TO THANK THE WOMEN WHO CONTRIBUTED THEIR STORIES: Amanda Abarbanel-Rice, Heather Chaplin, Nancy De Los Santos Reza, Gail Kass, Alex Leo, Geralyn Lucas, Merrill Markoe, Holly Millea, Stephanie Mnookin, Anne Navasky, Pamela Newton, Rosie O'Donnell, Shira Piven, Mary Rodgers, Elizabeth Segal, Nancy Short, Alex Witchel, Lisa Zeiler.

PRODUCTION NOTES

In the original production, the five actresses sat on high stools with backs, and their scripts were in three-hole binders on music stands. Gingy was stage right next to a coat rack on which the illustrations hung on hangers. They were reproduced on pieces of white posterboard, each measuring 22 inches wide by 35 inches long. A stagehand moved the appropriate illustration from the back to the front of the coat rack. At the beginning of the play, the title card is displayed in front of the other illustrations. When Gingy drew her own dress, she held a blank piece of posterboard and used a thick black marker pen.

All the actresses should wear black, as should the stagehand.

The Clotheslines and the Madonna piece were performed by all the actresses except for Gingy.

The play can be performed using five actresses, or more, and the parts can be assigned appropriate to age, girth, and so forth.

The illustrations for the play are available from Dramatists Play Service. The MetroCard bag can be purchased from the Transit Museum Store: transitmuseumstore.com.

LOVE, LOSS AND WHAT I WORE was first produced at the Westside Theater in New York City on October 1, 2009. It was directed by Karen L. Carpenter and produced by Daryl Roth; the set design was by Jo Winiarski; the costume design was by Jessica Jahn; the lighting design was by Jeff Croiter; and the sound design was by Walter Trarbach. The cast was as follows:

GINGY .... Tyne Daly
GINGY'S MOTHER, NANCY'S MOTHER,
ROSIE, LYNNE, MARY, NORA, DOCTOR .... Rosie O'Donnell
NANCY, STEPHANIE, LIZ, ANNIE,
EVE'S SHRINK, WOMAN, AMAND .... Samantha Bee
ALEX'S MOTHER, HOLLY, MERRILL,
OLDER SISTER, PAM, DORA,
EVE, LISA, GERALYN .... Katie Finneran
ALEX, NANCY ("The Gang Sweater"),
YOUNGER SISTER, MARY'S MOTHER,
HEATHER .... Natasha Lyonne

CHARACTERS

GINGY

GINGY'S MOTHER

NANCY

ALEX

NANCY'S MOTHER

ALEX'S MOTHER

ROSIE

HOLLY

STEPHANIE

NANCY ("The Gang Sweater")

MERILL

PAM

LYNNE

LIZ

Liz's OLDER SISTER

Liz's YOUNGER SISTER

DORA

ANNIE

MARY

EVE

MARY'S MOTHER

EVE'S SHRINK

HEATHER

NORA

LISA

AMANDA

GERALYN

DOCTOR

WOMAN

LOVE, LOSS, AND WHAT I WORE

SCENE 1

Gingy's Story

GINGY. One day, I was lying in bed with a backache, and I started thinking about a dress I used to wear. I drew a picture of it. Then I thought of another one. I decided to draw the dresses to hold onto them and when I finished, I thought, "These dresses tell a story." *(Gingy's drawings are hanging on a coat rack, and the first is revealed — a Brownie uniform.)* My Brownie uniform. My mother was our Brownie leader at Hunter College Elementary School on 69th Street between Lexington and Park. Even though she was our Brownie leader, she never got a Brownie leader's uniform. It was too expensive. *(A dress coat with leggings and mittens.)* A handmade brown dress coat with matching leggings and galoshes.
GINGY'S MOTHER. Gingy, put on your leggings —
GINGY. I hated putting on my leggings, which were held up by suspenders, and I always had a tantrum. *(As a child.)* I won't.
GINGY'S MOTHER. You have to put on your leggings, if you're going to play in the snow.
GINGY. *(As a child.)* No I don't.
GINGY'S MOTHER. If you don't, you know what will happen? You'll get polio.
GINGY. *(As an adult again.)* You can't imagine how many ways there were to get polio. You could get it from swimming pools and drinking water and, most terrifying of all, from swallowing a fly. *(Beat.)* Note the brightly-colored mittens. My mother was always knitting mittens for my sister and me. We lived at 333 East 66th Street, between First and Second Avenue, in a first-floor railroad flat

that faced the front. *(A green dress.)* My mother made this forest green wool jersey dress embroidered with red cherries for my sister. My sister's name was Blossom, but everyone called her Tootsie. Everybody called me Gingy because I was born with ginger-colored hair. *(Gingy's mother in a fox stole.)* My mother was a large, handsome woman who didn't wear fancy clothes, maybe because we couldn't afford them. Once my grandmother surprised her with a silver fox stole for her birthday or Mother's Day, I can't remember which. My mother tried it on, but she never wore it after that day. She usually wore a dark print dress and brown shoes with a buckle. She wore glasses, but whenever I draw her picture, I always forget to draw the glasses. Her face had the most beautiful shape. *(A black taffeta outfit.)* My mother made this black taffeta outfit, too. She made almost all of my sister's and my clothes. I wore this dress to dancing school at Ballet Arts in the Carnegie Hall building on 57th Street. I liked it very much, but what I really wanted was a store-bought outfit. *(Beat.)* Sometimes I would take the crosstown bus to Ballet Arts by myself. My mother would walk me to the bus.

GINGY'S MOTHER. Gingy, what is that smell?

GINGY. *(As a 12-year-old.)* What smell?

GINGY'S MOTHER. You know perfectly well what smell.

GINGY. *(As an adult.)* It was perfume. It was Tabu. I smelled like —

GINGY'S MOTHER. You smell like a bordello. You are too young to wear perfume.

GINGY. *(As a 12-year-old.)* Tootsie wears perfume.

GINGY'S MOTHER. Tootsie is seventeen. You are only twelve years old, you're still a baby —

GINGY. *(As a 12-year-old.)* I am not a baby —

GINGY'S MOTHER. And you smell so sweet without it. When you were a little girl, I used to just bury my head in your neck and inhale —

GINGY. — She used to just bury her head in my neck and inhale. *(A beat.)* The spring after my mother died, my father took me to B. Altman's department store on Fifth Avenue to buy a dress for my thirteenth birthday. We were both so sad, but when we got to the teen department my father said, "This is my daughter Gingy, she needs something to wear for her thirteenth birthday, and we need help." Everyone rushed to help us because he was so handsome. He was six feet tall. *(Two blue dresses.)* I picked two navy blue dresses and couldn't decide between them; I was in agony, so he said, "You don't have to decide, because you know what? I'm buying them both." He made them gift wrap them. This was a long time ago, when you didn't have to pay extra to have things gift-wrapped. Each dress was very expensive, about forty-four dollars. I wore this one to my thirteenth birthday party. *(Beat.)* One day my grandmother came and got my sister and me. She'd decided we were going to live with her and Grandpa and my Aunt Babbie. I never saw my father again.

SCENE 2

My Mother ...

NANCY. When I was thirteen —
ALEX. When I was thirteen —
NANCY. My mother went to Montreal —
ALEX. New York City —
NANCY and ALEX. And she brought me back —
NANCY. Not a twin set of adorable cashmere sweaters —
ALEX. Not a CPO, which was a jacket that looked like a shirt made out of black wool and I wanted one so badly —
NANCY. Not a pair of Capezios —
ALEX. Or bell-bottom jeans, which had just come in and everyone had them but me — but instead —
NANCY. A pair of socks.
ALEX. An Outfit.
NANCY. The loudest ugliest long socks.
ALEX. No one was wearing Outfits.
NANCY. They were striped ...
ALEX. My whole class at Scarsdale High School was dressing like hippies and she gave me an Outfit. For my birthday.
NANCY. The socks were meant to be worn —
NANCY'S MOTHER. Mid-thigh —
NANCY. Mid-thigh, she said. And they were French —
NANCY'S MOTHER. They're from Paris —
NANCY. Cigarette-smoking, finger-thin Frenchies wore them —
NANCY'S MOTHER. They're *très chic* —

NANCY. And I was not thin, did I mention that? And they were striped ...

NANCY'S MOTHER. Everyone is wearing them.

NANCY. They are?

ALEX. Brown plaid wool pants, an ivory silk blouse with a bow tie, and a crocheted vest just to pull it all together. I went ballistic. *(To her mother.)* What is this? I can't believe you bought me this. I hate this.

ALEX'S MOTHER. What's wrong with it?

ALEX. Everything. What have I ever done to make you think I would ever even put this "outfit" on. It looks like something you would wear.

ALEX'S MOTHER. I only wish I could wear something like that. It's a beautiful —

ALEX. Outfit. Like anyone wears outfits.

ALEX'S MOTHER. At least try it on. *(Beat.)* You look adorable.

ALEX. I do not. I'm taking it back.

ALEX'S MOTHER. You can't take it back.

ALEX. Why not? *(A beat.)* Because it was on sale? You bought me a birthday present that was on sale? What if I didn't like it, which I don't? *(She bursts into tears.)*

ALEX'S MOTHER. You are an ungrateful girl. You are a horrible, ungrateful girl. You don't appreciate anything.

ALEX. My life is over. Just from wearing it in the house.

ALEX'S MOTHER. Fine.

ALEX. Fine!

ALEX'S MOTHER. I'll never buy you anything again.

ALEX. Good! I don't care. *(To audience.)* The next year on my birthday, she gave me a paperback copy of *Between Parent and Child* and a frozen Sara Lee banana cake, because "I didn't appreciate anything anyway." *(Beat.)* My mother.

NANCY'S MOTHER. You look adorable.

NANCY. Do I?

NANCY'S MOTHER. The French have the best sense of style.

NANCY. *(To audience.)* So the next day I put on my new socks and got on my bike to go to school, and I felt very daring and *très chic* for a quarter of a mile, until I passed Michael Sherman, the boy I had been in love with for two years. And the second I saw him and he started laughing, I knew it was all wrong, Mom had completely deceived me, she never had a clue about style. So of course big laughs behind my back all day long. Even one of my teachers said something.

It was bad. And the worst thing was, when I told my mom, when I sobbed about how humiliated I was, she thought it was funny.

NANCY'S MOTHER. *(She laughs.)* Honey, if you wear them again tomorrow, everyone will think it's the new trend. That's how trends start, you know?

NANCY. My mother.

SCENE 3

Clothesline: What My Mother Said

Don't wear stripes and prints together.

Loafers ruin your feet.

Stop tugging at your crotch, Samantha.

If you wear a girdle, you will destroy your stomach muscles.

Always wear clean underpants in case you die in a car accident.

You never wear that dress. Do you know how much I paid for it?

Never buy a red coat ...

I saw your friend Stephanie at the mall. Is she wearing the blouse I bought you?

Go right back upstairs and take that off.

Nice Jewish girls do not get their ears pierced.

You'd be so pretty if you —

Lost weight —

Gained weight —

Didn't make faces —

Fixed your nose —

Cut your hair —

Combed your hair —

Washed your hair —

Kept your hair out of your eyes —

Stood up straight —

Ate fruit —

Put on a little lipstick —

Took off all that makeup.

Aw, honey, you look so beautiful.

Just looking at you, I'm going to cry.

My little baby is all grown up.

You're so pretty.

Do you know how pretty you are?

You're pretty enough for all normal purposes.

Is that what you're wearing?

Are you wearing that deliberately to annoy me?

Never wear white before Memorial Day.

Never wear white after Labor Day.

Never wear white.

You're much too young to wear black.

Never wear black pants with a white shirt or you'll look like the caterer's help.

Never wear velvet before Rosh Hashanah.

What did you do to your hair?

Is that a tattoo?

If you wear that, you're going to be sent home for breaking the dress code.

Take that off, you look like a slut.

You look like a prostitute.

You look like a gypsy.

You look like a bag lady.

You look like a waitress in a Hungarian restaurant.

I don't understand. You could look so good if you just tried.

I don't know why I buy you things.

A tiara? … You want a tiara? Where are you planning to wear a tiara?

Your bra strap is showing … What do you mean, it's supposed to show?

SCENE 4

The Bathrobe

ROSIE. The truth is, I have no fashion sense — never did. For many years I blamed this on my mom's death. Then again, I blame pretty much everything on that — my weight, my addiction to television, my inability to spell. In my fantasy world, had my mother lived, I would be extremely well-dressed. I would know what went with what, and everything I tried on would fit. Mom and I would shop together at the places that moms and daughters go — a department store, an outlet mall, the flea market. I would wear a lot of tasteful makeup too. We would lunch someplace while shopping. It would be at a café where we would have salad and like it. We'd laugh about how great our lives turned out and make plans for all the things we were still going to do. But that's all a dream, because my mother did not live. She died when she was 39 years old. *(Beat.)* The fact is that no item of clothing has ever moved me in any way — except one. After my mom died, my dad took his five motherless children to Belfast, Northern Ireland. I guess he thought we could best recover from the trauma of her death by living in a war zone. The IRA was nowhere near as scary as what had just happened to our lives. When we returned, we found her side of the closet empty. All her clothes were gone. *(Beat.)* A few years later my dad got remarried to a lovely woman. She was a schoolteacher named Mary May. After the wedding she moved in. That first morning she was there, I was eating breakfast with a few of my siblings when my new stepmom walked down the stairs and into the kitchen. She was wearing a long burgundy velour three-quarter sleeve zip bathrobe with a thick vertical white stripe down the center, surrounding the zipper. No one said a word. We all looked at each other then back at Mary as she happily made her way to the stove to put on the kettle. My mother had had the same exact bathrobe — in blue. Electric blue. What are the chances of that really? The unspoken rule in my house was that my mom's name was never mentioned after her death. But that morning, I knew that rule was about to be broken. My siblings left the kitchen. I was

14

alone with Mary. "Mary," I said. "My mom had that same bathrobe in blue," "Oh," she said. And that robe disappeared. Gone. Sent away to the same place my mother's clothes went, I assume. *(Beat.)* To this day that bathrobe is the only piece of clothing I can actually see in my mind. I have no visuals of prom dresses or favorite sweater or shoes I couldn't live without. Clothes are just something I use for cover, leaving room for one electric blue memory.

SCENE 5

Holly's Story

HOLLY. If I could draw, I would draw you the dress my mother gave me when I was five years old. It was my favorite dress ever. It had long sleeves, and it was charcoal gray wool with a big lace pilgrim collar and a black satin bow in the center and lace cuffs. A few months after my mother gave it to me, my father, who was a doctor, sent my mother away to a mental hospital, moved his nurse into our house, divorced my mother, and married the nurse. We had a cleaning lady who came in once a week who had a daughter a little younger than me, and my stepmother used to give her my hand-me-downs. One day I couldn't find my beautiful dress. I asked my stepmother if she'd seen it. "It will turn up," she said. A week later, I went to school, and during recess I found my dress, on the cleaning lady's daughter. I could not believe it. I ran up to her and grabbed her by the collar screaming, "That's MY dress, MY dress, MY dress" again and again until the recess monitor pulled us apart. The little girl stood there, shaking and crying. And I stood there shaking and crying, holding my satin bow in my fist. I wasn't punished because the school "understood." But I remember wishing that they had punished me. Shame on me. And my stepmother too.

SCENE 6

Gingy's Story: Part 2

GINGY. We lived with my grandparents in a brownstone building at 743 Madison Avenue between 65th and 66th Streets. They owned the stationery store on the street level. It was called Harry Goldberg's. We lived above the store. *(Gingy's grandmother.)* My grandmother. My grandmother had very beautiful long silver-gray hair that she twisted up on top of her head into a bun. She believed in two cures: hot tea for anything wrong inside the body, and Vaseline for anything wrong outside the body. Here's what she always said: "It's as easy to fall in love with a rich man as a poor man." Which isn't true. Why do people say that? It's not true. My Aunt Babbie had enormous breasts. Once I saw her naked and it scared me to death. *(Gingy's friend Dora in a middy blouse.)* My best friend Dora. She had a beauty mark at the end of her eyebrow. Dora lived at 22 East 65th Street, right across the street from me, and we used to lean out of our windows and shout down things at men who were walking past, like "Hey, mister — you're going bald." We thought we were hilarious. Dora's mother was a dress designer for rich ladies. Whenever Dora went someplace special, her mother would say, "Take Gingy along." *(A satin evening gown.)* She lent me this peach satin strapless gown when Dora and I went to the Choate School for Boys in Connecticut for the weekend. The preppy girls gave us mean looks and called us whores, probably because we spent the entire weekend necking with our dates. *(A coral wool jersey dress.)* This is the coral wool jersey dress I bought for a date with Walter Fenton. I was madly in love with Walter Fenton. Every time we'd go out, Walter begged me to go all the way. Finally, at a fraternity party at Dartmouth Winter Carnival, he told me that he couldn't see me anymore because necking was just too painful. He went off to have a beer and left me sitting on the floor. After a long time he came back and said he was going to drive me back to the place where I was supposed to sleep, but I said I didn't want to, I wanted to spend the night with him. "Are you sure?" he said. "I'm sure," I said. So we did it. That's when I found out that in sex, once you do something you have to keep doing it. At the end of my freshman year, I thought I was pregnant. I had no idea what to do, so I went to my sociology professor at Simmons College for advice. He had taught a class in Marriage and the Family and I thought he could help me. It turned out I wasn't pregnant. But by then, Walter had vanished.

SCENE 7

Clothesline: The Bra

That is such a painful subject.

My first bra.

I can't even talk about my first bra.

May Company.

Macy's.

Nordstrom's.

Bloomingdale's at a bra sale and I was almost trampled to death.

My father took me. I still can't talk about it.

Bras, breasts, the whole works, this is a very painful subject.

I was always trying on bras.

My aunt had this really big one and I used to wear it on my head.

My first bra was like two triangles. I got it at Jordan Marsh. It was awful, because there was some really cute guy there shopping with his girlfriend and my mom kept saying, "Julia, why are you in that section? The training bras are over here."

My mother said, "If you don't wear a bra you will get pendulum breasts."

It was a 28AA bra. Tiny, but not tiny enough. I put it on and there were like empty little puffs on my chest. The saleswoman said, "Lean over." So I leaned over, hoping that breasts would magically tumble out of my body and into the bra. But they didn't.

I bought a blow-up bra. It had plastic balloon inserts and came with a plastic straw that you inserted into the balloons and blew up to the size you wanted. One day I was talking to this guy I had a crush on, and one side collapsed right before his eyes.

It was something about your dad.

You couldn't run around the house naked any more.

You couldn't sit on your daddy's lap.

The breasts, the bra, the divide.

My mom's friend worked at Bloomingdale's when I was in college and recommended the Minimizer. It's a spandex bra that flattens your boobs about a cup size. I was totally excited about it because I was so self-conscious about my breasts. The bra flattened me but kind of gave me a monoboob look. I wore it to the veterinary hospital where I was working as a technician. There was this crazy Indian substitute vet there. He said, "Please don't take this personally, this is only for your own good, but I have to say there is something wrong with your boob." I said, "I don't know you and I don't appreciate your comments about my boobs. They are none of your business." First time I ever stood up for my boobs.

Someone gave me a cashmere halter top that needs a bra to make it work. So I go to the Town Shop on Broadway and tell the saleswoman Marvelene my size. She immediately tells me I'm wrong. "All you girls think you should be going up in inches but you should be going up a cup." I am deposited in something that perhaps is a dressing room but looks like a utility closet with a mirror and a case of paper towels. I'm strapped into my strapless when the curtain is parted like the Red Sea and my linebacker saleswoman commands me to bend over. She then grabs me and my bra and hoists us up until I can feel the blood changing direction in my body. She reaches in, cups my breasts with her hands and shifts them. Then she invites all the other saleswomen in to look at me. Everyone cheers. I look in the mirror. I realize that I am a new woman and it took Marvelene feeling me up in a utility closet to get me this way.

SCENE 8

The Prom Dress

STEPHANIE. My junior prom dress was powder blue and white. It was ribbed, with tiny ribs and a white waistband and a white band around the bottom kind of like Cinderella, with a big powder blue bow. The problem was my date. He rang the bell, and I opened the door, and there he was, in a powder blue tuxedo with a white frilly shirt and a powder blue bow tie. We matched. It was totally mortifying. I didn't really like him but I was sort of the last to be asked to the prom — not the very last but one of the last, so I didn't really have a choice in the date or in what he wore, and I had a really horrible time at the prom, and afterwards we went into a field and tipped cows. *(Beat.)* My senior prom was completely different. My prom dress was black and short, it was in that sort of Madonna 1980s style, her "Like a Virgin" phase, tight on top and then it went out in a black net pouf and black lace gloves. My date was also short, but dark and handsome, and we ended up drinking champagne and making out in his car, and it was great. But here's the thing — I've never really known for sure which of those two people I am — the girl who almost doesn't get asked to the prom at all or the girl who gets to go with a really cute guy. Every time I thought I knew which one I was, I turned out to be the other. Which is one reason why I think I got married, to, like, end the confusion.

SCENE 9

Madonna

Any American woman under the age of thirty who says she's never dressed as Madonna is either lying or Amish.

Madonna represents sexual freedom —

Third-wave feminism —

Individuality —

And fabulous fashion.

Last year, for Halloween, we all dressed as Madonna from four different stages of her career.

I was *Desperately Seeking Susan* Madonna. I wore a black T-shirt cut to reveal my stomach, silver necklaces tied in lariats, a huge black skirt and red Converse sneakers.

I was "Blond Ambition Tour" Madonna. Tight black leotard, fishnet stockings, a headset, and this was really brilliant, two paper party hats I painted black to create a big black pointy bra.

I was "Express Yourself" Madonna. I wore a man's suit, rocked a red lip, and cut slashes in the suit jacket so my bra showed through.

I was "Patty" Hearst Madonna. I wore that cute little hat Patty wore when she robbed the bank, and a trench coat, and a fake gun strapped across my chest.

Anyway, these costumes, and a whole lot of cosmos, totally freed us.

I made out with a girl.

Oh my God, I made out with a bunch of gay men.

I practically got into a fistfight with another group of girls dressed as —

ALL. Madonna!

And whenever "Vogue" came on, we totally hit the floor. *(They all vogue.)*

ALL. Vogue. Vogue. Vogue. Vogue. Vogue.

SCENE 10

The Gang Sweater

NANCY. I felt so hot in my gang sweater. I was fifteen, and it was the first thing I'd had tailor-made for me — the only thing ever, now that I think about it. I'd joined this gang called The Latin Chantels. We were the *chicas* of The Latin Chancellors, the guys who hung out near the corner of 27th and Normal streets in Chicago. The sweater was hip-length and bad, black with royal blue trim around the collar and on the pockets. The best thing about it was the emblem, a big puffy rendition of some long-time-ago coat of arms that had been designed by Lemons, the War Lord of the Latin Chancellors. The emblem was sewed onto the sweater, near your heart. *(Beat.)* I wore my gang sweater with black stretch pants, the kind with the strap that goes under your feet. I knew I looked cool in that outfit. So cool that the first day I wore it, Lemons asked to walk me home. I could barely breathe. I was in heaven walking through the dark Chicago streets with Lemons at my side. I thrilled when he pulled me into a doorway and began kissing me. When he unbuttoned my sweater, I shuddered. When he put his hand under my blouse right under the emblem he had designed, I figured it was meant to be. Lemons never spoke to me after that day. He fell madly in love with Irma, the president of The Latin Capris. Their sweaters were black with purple trim. Cool.

SCENE 11

Boots

MERRILL. I got my first pair of boots when I was 14. They were suede, and they were the answer to my need to be identified as a brooding, wounded, but potentially brilliant artistic subspecies of female with practically no genetic relationship to my miserable screaming family. My dog Corky got them confused with an entree and ate a hole in them, so I took a bus to Sausalito and got a new pair. They were olive green leather and came up above my knees. By the time I got to Berkeley, where I was an art student, I was all boots all the time. Freshman year I had two pairs. One was golden brown, one was deeper brown, and I wore them with really, really short skirts. I thought my boots gave me a kind of mysterious, Bohemian charisma, tough but tender, rugged but sensuous, poetic but unself-conscious, like Joni Mitchell. It was a really happy time of my life, but then, one night, when I was sleeping, a guy broke into my apartment and raped me. They never caught him. I have no reason at all to think that he'd ever seen me before that night. But after the rape, when I walked down the streets of Berkeley in my boots and my short skirt, it suddenly seemed like everyone was staring at me. So I gave my short skirts to Goodwill. But not the boots. I love boots.

SCENE 12

Clothesline: The Dressing Room

What do you think?

Does this go in or out?

What is this length?

I can't even zip it up.

The only reason I can't zip this up is I have my period.

Omigod, I'm up a size.

This will fit if I lose five pounds.

This will fit if I lose ten pounds.

This will fit if I have lipo.

This doesn't fit.

Do you think this can be let out?

This doesn't fit now, but I always lose weight in May.

I don't know who this is cut for.

But I'm a 6. I've always been a 6.

Does this come in an 8?

Does this come in a 12?

Does this come in a 14-slash-16?

Does this make me look pregnant?

I can't decide.

What color is this?

I can't wear gray.

Yellow makes me look sick.

I look so pale in green.

It's so red.

It's so red.

Is this black or navy blue?

I can't buy another black turtleneck sweater.

I can't buy another white T-shirt.

I look like my mother.

What am I supposed to wear with this?

Does this match?

If you're not buying that could I try it on?

Does this run small?

Is there something wrong with the lighting in here?

Is this mirror, like, distorted?

It doesn't fit.

I can't wear anything without sleeves.

I can't wear anything lowcut.

My arms. What happened to my arms?

If my elbows faced forward, I would kill myself.

My butt is falling.

Is my butt falling?

Omigod my butt fell.

Does this make me look fat?

Tell me the truth.

I can't decide.

I can't decide.

I can't decide.

I can't decide.

SCENE 13

The Shirt

PAM. Last summer I lost my favorite shirt. Or to be more accurate, my favorite shirt vanished into thin air. When I got home from being away for the summer and I unpacked my bags, the shirt simply never materialized. I have replayed the sequence of events in my mind several times, and I have theories about what happened to it, but the fact remains that the shirt just ceased to be. The really sad part was that this came at the end of a summer when that shirt gradually revealed itself to be the perfect shirt. It was flattering (I always felt pretty in it), I liked the color and the cut, it went with all my favorite pants, it was casual and dressed down but not crappy and falling apart, it was comfortable. It was one of those shirts you have to make yourself NOT wear, because it seems every day's outfit would be improved by it. And as silly as it may sound, I am generally happier when I have clothes like this in my life, when there's something I know I can put on and feel good in. Something to fall back on. When I realized the shirt was gone, I couldn't think of anything else I owned that served remotely the same function, and I felt cheated out of something truly rare and precious.

I realize that I sound like I'm talking about death, or about lost love — and maybe I am. It's probably worth noting that my relationship with my boyfriend was ending at just the same time I lost the shirt. But I could have sworn to you at the time that I was not transferring my feelings about the loss of my boyfriend onto the shirt, but was actually mourning the loss of the shirt itself. The main lesson to be learned from this experience came from the purchase of eight different shirts, which each had some likeness to the lost shirt, whether it be in color, cut, material, casualness. But none of them in any way replaced it, and I eventually had to resolve to be thankful for the time I had with the shirt and move on. At least I know what I'm looking for.

SCENE 14

Gingy's Story: Part 3

Pink satin dress.

GINGY. Pink satin princess-style dress I bought in Filene's Basement in Boston for my marriage to Harry M. Johnson. I was twenty and Harry was thirty-seven. Harry was my sociology professor at Simmons. We were married at his best friend's house in Dobbs Ferry. There was no food, only champagne and wedding cake. My grandmother and Aunt Babbie came to the wedding. My grandfather wouldn't come because he thought Harry was too old for me and besides he was Catholic. Here are the words my grandmother uttered on this occasion: "You're killing me." *(Beat.)* One day I was coming down the front steps from our apartment and there was Walter Fenton. He had joined the navy. He looked handsomer than ever in his uniform. "Gingy," he said. "Why did you do it?" He kissed my cheek and then my hand and walked away. I would love to be able to tell you that nothing good ever happened to Walter Fenton, that he ended up being a used-car salesman, but the truth is, he won a Pulitzer Prize, the prick. *(Chinese dinner dress.)* Iridescent-brocade Chinese-style dinner dress I bought in Cambridge for a New Year's Eve party. Harry convinced me to buy this dress even though it was expensive. He said it showed off my arms. He thought my arms were pretty. The party was at the home of Harry's friends Penny and Ecky. They were married. I idolized Penny. She carried a diaphragm in her purse, which was very cool but strange, I wondered about it at the time, because isn't the whole point of getting married that you don't have to carry your diaphragm in your purse? Anyway, at midnight, I got very upset because I couldn't find Harry. Then I saw him. He was kissing Penny. "Harry!" I said. And you know what he said? Of course you know what he said. He said, "It's not what you think." But it was exactly what I thought. So that was that. I was twenty-one years old and I was going to be the youngest divorced person in America, except for Elizabeth Taylor.

SCENE 15

Lynne's Story

LYNNE. In the beginning, I remember the jewelry more than the clothes. When I met Ray, we were both married, and we worked at the same truck dealership, and he used to say that falling in love with me was like lettuce. Because when he was a kid he had colitis, and for a long time he wasn't allowed to eat any roughage, and he missed it a lot. When he finally was allowed to have it, his mother introduced it slowly, a little bit of lettuce at a time, and he described eating that first plate of lettuce almost like a religious experience, relishing the look, the smell, the sound and the taste. Like he was coming alive. So the first gift he gave me was a ring he had made that spelled LETTUCE. L-E-T-T-U-C-E. Still have it, it's a little bit tight. Anyway, even before we slept together he told me about how he was in trouble, he'd been arrested, he was probably going to jail, and then he told me all over again because he wanted to make sure he hadn't misled me. But all I could think about was how much I wanted to go to bed with him. And I wasn't shocked that he was going to jail because remember, I'm a Gorman. My family was always doing "things." My grandmother and my mother were arrested for making gin in the bathtub, my Auntie Bernice, who was a policewoman, was thrown off the Baltimore Police Abortion

Squad for arranging abortions, and my cousin Davey faked his own funeral to get out of his car payments.

So Ray and I, we fell in love and he left his wife, I left my husband, and Ray was sentenced to seven years, but thank God at a minimum security prison. I went up to visit him every weekend. Sometimes I wore a special pair of pants I had, loose-fitting brown cotton, and I made a hole in the crotch for easy access by Ray's finger. Obviously Ray didn't get much from this except the satisfaction of pleasing me, but he always wanted to show me that even in jail he could take better care of me than someone who was not in jail. And of course we wanted to hold on to freedom, put something over on the guards, get away with it, that was the best part. Because they were so horrible when they cleared you in, they frisked you, they went through your bag like they controlled you, which they did. Ray got out of prison after two and a half years, and I picked him up that day wearing a pair of knee-high caramel colored boots and a raincoat. Ray comes down and he looks at me and there was a grin from ear to ear because he knew I had nothing on underneath and the guards didn't know. *(Beat.)* And by the way, we just celebrated our twentieth wedding anniversary. I'm a state senator. Ray is a life coach. He coaches people on their life. If you lived where we live, you'd know us. But you wouldn't know the story.

SCENE 16

Sisters

LIZ. I always wanted a pair of black cowboy boots. I thought they'd make me sort of rangy and taller, like a girl named Slim that a guy could really go for. So one day I wandered into Walker's Western Wear and bought a pair of Noconas. Beautiful stitching on the side, shit-kicker pointy toes. $250. The salesman said they'd be good for my arches. I have terrible arches.
OLDER SISTER. She's obsessed with her arches.
LIZ. My older sister.
YOUNGER SISTER. She's always been obsessed with her arches.
LIZ. My younger sister. *(Beat.)* A month later, I met a guy I fell in

love with, Chase. He owned six pairs of black cowboy boots, not Noconas, but still really nice Tony Lamas. As fate would have it, he turned out to be the same sexy guy I'd just seen standing against a Doric column at a party at the architecture school.

OLDER SISTER. It was Halloween, don't leave that out.

YOUNGER SISTER. He had a chainsaw through his torso.

OLDER SISTER. How could she resist him?

YOUNGER SISTER. She couldn't.

LIZ. He was a sort of freckly prepster and since I was freckly too, there we were, meant to be, with our freckles and black boots, skinny freckly arms all entangled.

OLDER SISTER. She followed him to Seattle.

LIZ. He invited me.

SISTERS. No he did not.

LIZ. One of the reasons he wanted to move west was to get away from his incredibly dysfunctional family in Connecticut. Although if I ever said his family was dysfunctional, he would say — "Hold it right there. My family is not dysfunctional. If you want to talk about dysfunctional families, what about your family?"

OLDER SISTER. "What about your sisters?"

YOUNGER SISTER. "What about your sisters who hate me?"

OLDER SISTER. Which we did.

YOUNGER SISTER. Because of the way he treated her.

OLDER SISTER. Although she let him, he couldn't have behaved like that if she hadn't let him.

YOUNGER SISTER. We discussed it for hours.

OLDER SISTER. Behind her back.

YOUNGER SISTER. What a jerk he was.

OLDER SISTER. Why is she in love with him?

YOUNGER SISTER. Why?

OLDER SISTER. Why?

YOUNGER SISTER. Why? *(Beat.)*

LIZ. Where was I?

OLDER SISTER. His incredibly dysfunctional family.

LIZ. Right. So he said …

YOUNGER SISTER. "If you're going to insult my family, I'm outta here."

OLDER SISTER. And she said —

LIZ. "Don't go. Please don't go. Please. Don't go. I didn't mean it. I love you."

YOUNGER SISTER. "I love you."

OLDER SISTER. "I love you."

YOUNGER SISTER. He was always threatening to leave —

OLDER SISTER. And every time she said —

LIZ. "Don't go. Please don't go. Please. Don't go. I didn't mean it. I love you."

YOUNGER SISTER. So, guess what? He stayed.

LIZ. After a while I began to suspect that he was actually in love with his family and not really with me at all. He'd go home for the holidays without me bearing gifts I'd helped him shop for, and he'd come back with old Shetland sweaters that reminded him of his childhood — but what I really wanted was for him to come back with the realization that he'd missed me horribly, he couldn't live without me, he wanted to marry me, he loved me, or failing any of that, at least that he someday wanted me to meet his fucking parents. Which I finally told him, in those very words —

OLDER SISTER. And he said —

YOUNGER SISTER. "If you're going to insult my family I'm outta here."

OLDER SISTER. And she said —

LIZ. "Fine."

OLDER SISTER. Isn't that amazing?

LIZ. "Fine. Go. Split. Who cares? And take those fucking boots with you."

OLDER SISTER. And he left.

YOUNGER SISTER. Just like that.

LIZ. After seven years and seven horrible Christmases. At which point, he owned about twelve pairs of Tony Lamas, most of them with holes, and I still had my own well-oiled, well cared-for pair of Noconas. He kept the Shetland sweaters and his childhood memories. And I left town. And found a good shrink. In Los Angeles —

SISTERS. Where we live.

SCENE 17

Clothesline: The Closet

I have nothing to wear.

Nothing.

Nothing fits.

Nothing fits me!

Why did I buy this piece of shit?

Where is it?

Why can't I find anything in my closet?

I hate my clothes.

Why do I buy such terrible clothes?

I have to clean out my closet.

I absolutely have to.

I should throw this away. After all, if I haven't worn it in two years —

Three years —

Five years —

I can't do it.

My mother gave me this. Who does she think I am?

I can't find my black turtleneck sweater.

Where is it?

I can't find it!

Now I'm sweating!

Why didn't I hang this up? Now I have to iron it.

I have nothing to wear.

Who bought this?

Who did I think I was when I bought this?

I totally forgot I bought this.

Do men ever go through this — choosing the sweater, unchoosing the sweater, choosing the sweater, unchoosing the sweater?

Of course they don't.

What's wrong with me?

WHERE IS IT?

I have nothing to wear.

I have nothing to wear.

I have nothing to wear.

Nothing.

SCENE 18

Gingy's Story: Part 4

GINGY. After I got divorced, I moved back to New York and lived with Dora, who was studying to be an actress.

DORA. Gingy, you are the second-youngest divorced person in the world and you must act as if you couldn't care less —

GINGY. I had no idea what Dora meant —

DORA. What I mean is, don't marry the first person you go out with just so you can stop being divorced.

GINGY. Don't be ridiculous. Why would I do that?

DORA. Are you listening to me, Gingy? *(A yellow wool dress.)*

GINGY. This is a yellow ochre sack dress Dora lent me when she fixed me up with Al Beckerman.

DORA. He's very sweet, but don't marry him. Are you listening to me, Gingy? *(A floral print pique dress.)*

GINGY. Floral-print cotton pique dress I purchased at a very snooty store in New Canaan, Connecticut, for my marriage to Al Beckerman. My grandmother and Babbie came to the wedding, but my grandfather wouldn't come. He was still mad at me for marrying Harry. Al was so sweet — He's very sweet, I said to Dora, and she said —

DORA. I know, he's very sweet, but are you sure?

GINGY. *(To Dora.)* He'll take care of me —

DORA. I know, but are you sure?

GINGY. *(To Dora.)* We both want a big family.

DORA. How big, Gingy? *(A maternity dress.)*

GINGY. Black and red print taffeta maternity dress, first worn when I was pregnant with Isabelle, and then when I was pregnant with Lillie, Michael, Joe, Julie, and David. David died when he was eighteen months old from a forty-eight-hour intestinal virus. "Your son has expired," they said when they called from the hospital. "Your son has expired." *(Beat.)* After David died, everything changed. *(A beige wool pants suit.)* I ordered this beige wool pants suit from the Spiegel catalogue. It was my first mail-order purchase. I thought it would be a good interview outfit because, now that the children were all in school, I wanted to go to work. I got a job at an ad agency. One day I walked into my office and a man was sitting at my desk. He had a glue stick in his hand. He said: "Do you know how to open this fucking thing?" It was as if Cupid had shot an arrow right into my heart. "Fuck" he said, and left. Later that day I found out his name was Stanley. So there it was. First Walter, then Harry, then Al, then Stanley. *(A Diane von Furstenberg dress.)* I loved this print jersey Diane von Furstenberg wrap dress. It was easy to put on and very comfortable and if you gained a few pounds it still fit. I was wearing it the day I told Al I couldn't stay married to him any more because I'd fallen in love with Stanley. It wasn't really Al's fault. Al was so sweet.

SCENE 19

Annie's Story

ANNIE. There was, for a very brief moment in time, the paper dress. And I had one. I got it at Paraphernalia, which was Betsy Johnson's first store, on 67th and Madison. It was a kind of greyish plaid sheath. I wore it to brunch at my cousin Marty's. He was an advertising executive who had just married Steffie, whom he put through medical school and then she ran off with a doctor. They were very impressed with my dress and how au courant I was. Then I wore it to Paula's sister Janet's and her new husband Earl's, who invited me and Paula to dinner at their newlywed apartment which contained their newly-upholstered dining room chairs. In the middle of dinner, I got my period suddenly and violently. And when we all stood up, there was a blood stain on the seat of one of the prized new chairs. For history I should say that the dress was completely intact, just wet. It must have been the predecessor to Bounty paper towels. Anyway, when I stood up, Janet said something like, "WHAAT???" and I said something like "What?" As though nothing had happened at all. I then left the room for the bathroom. God knows what the three of them did because I never acknowledged to anyone that anything out of the ordinary had happened. Although I will remember this on my deathbed.

SCENE 20

Fat/Thin

MARY. I started getting fat when I was 12.
EVE. I was always thin.
MARY. By the time I was 15, I was a size 20.
EVE. Not just thin, skinny. Which would not have mattered if I had had breasts, but I didn't.

MARY. If I ate a carrot, I gained three pounds.

MARY'S MOTHER. Mary, is that you in the refrigerator?

MARY. It was. My mother kept saying —

MARY'S MOTHER. You have a very pretty face, you could be attractive if you'd just lose weight.

MARY. My mother was the most competent human being alive but she gave up on me clothes-wise. She would send me off alone in a taxi to a store called Jane Engel on the southeast corner of 79th and Madison, and they'd bring me clothes and I'd try them on. There was a dressing room with three mirrors, and no matter which way I looked, there I was, big as a house. *(Beat.)* There has never ever been a good time to be fat, but this was a particularly bad time on account of Audrey Hepburn.

EVE. My shrink said —

EVE'S SHRINK. If you ever got happy you would gain weight.

EVE. And she also said —

EVE'S SHRINK. This is all because of your mother.

EVE. *(To the shrink.)* My mother? I'm thin because of my mother?

EVE'S SHRINK. Yes.

EVE. Couldn't it be my metabolism?

EVE'S SHRINK. No.

MARY. By the time I married Kenny, I managed to diet down to 152 pounds, which was rail-thin for me, but Kenny didn't care what I weighed because he was gay and he would have married me if I'd had two heads.

EVE. I have a picture of me and my first husband together, on a bench in Washington Square Park. I was wearing my lime green winter coat, so short, with a plaid scarf, and I look really happy. But I was never happy with David. Whenever I see that picture, I always think how photos lie and how many marriages are just performances.

MARY. When I married Kenny, I wore my mother's wedding dress, which fit with some adjustments. She'd bought it at Bergdorf's. It was an absolutely gorgeous dress, ivory satin, plain, with long sleeves with lace insets that came to a point, and a great long train. Just as I was getting into the dress before the wedding, the dressmaker pricked her finger on a needle, just like in *Sleeping Beauty,* and got blood on the dress. My mother said —

MARY'S MOTHER. I know how to fix that.

MARY. And she did. After all, she was the most competent human being alive. She got an ice cube, and out came the bloodstain. I wore the dress at my wedding, my sister wore it at hers, my older daughter wore it at hers, until finally it got down to my younger daughter Jenny who said, "No way in hell am I getting into that bad luck dress." So we had a wedding dress designed for her by Vera Wang, and Jenny got divorced too. We all got divorced, my whole family, everyone except my mother who stayed married to my father for fifty-six miserable years.

EVE. After I was married to David for three years, I began to end-lessly fantasize about tragically and miraculously losing him. Every time he was five minutes late, automobile accident. Every time he coughed, TB. Every time we went to a party I hoped that he would go into the kitchen and kiss one of my girlfriends and run off with her, but none of them really liked him.

EVE'S SHRINK. You are ambivalent.

EVE. Ambivalent? I was not remotely ambivalent —

EVE'S SHRINK. You are ambivalent. You really love him — you are just too neurotic to realize it.

EVE. I was neurotic. But not because I didn't love my husband — because I was pretending to love my husband when I didn't. *(Beat.)* After six years David and I split up, but not before spending an entire week talking nonstop. We even ended up talking naked, which you might imagine meant that we finally spoke the truth, but we did not.

EVE'S SHRINK. Why were you naked?

EVE. Because we'd just had sex. We were lying there and my hus-band was telling me he wanted me to stop writing. I had hardly written anything at that point, I'd written one book, *The Adventurous Crocheter*, and I remember while he was talking to me, I recited the beginning of it to myself so I wouldn't hear anything he was saying. "There is no wrong way to crochet. There are easier ways and harder ways, but there is no wrong way to crochet." So David and I got divorced. And I left my shrink. *(To shrink.)* I mean, fuck you.

MARY. When I married Henry, I wore my mother's navy blue suit. I looked like a one hundred-and-ten-year-old Italian war widow, but I lived happily ever after.

EVE. When I married Jerry, I wore a shocking pink Mexican cot-ton skirt and a white Mexican blouse, off the shoulder. It wasn't the sort of thing that would look good on a skinny person, but I'd gained five pounds, and we all know what a big deal five pounds is.

SCENE 21

Shoes

HEATHER. I look gorgeous in high heels. Everyone looks gorgeous in high heels. But my feet hurt. My little toe was always crushed. I had a bunion. I was in so much pain, I couldn't think. I had to choose — heels or think. *(Beat.)* I chose think. *(Beat.)* So I bought some chic flat shoes. I made a lot of mistakes. I bought these turquoise blue Mark Jacobs ballet flats that the salesman talked me into because he said they had toe cleavage. I'd never heard of toe cleavage. Anyway I realized that chic flat shoes are almost as uncomfortable as heels, and don't do that amazing thing for your legs. *(Beat.)* Fortunately, at just about that time, I met an unbelievably stylish woman who was wearing Birkenstocks. When I was in high school, I was a Doc Martens girl, and Birkenstocks symbolized everything I didn't want to be. They were incredibly uncool and the girls who wore them had big dirty toes that stuck out the ends. You absolutely could not be friends with a person who wore Birkenstocks. But this stylish woman wore her Birks with baggy cords and a Comme de Garçons sleeveless shirt. It was a revelation. The next day I went out and got a pedicure and a pair — dark brown, standard style. I realized that Birkenstocks were actually the coolest punk-est shoes a girl could wear. They were a statement, "Look, these are my feet, we all have them. Okay?" My husband had a slightly different opinion. He hated my Birkenstocks. He said they made me look like a troll from Middle-Earth. And once, when the Yankees were in the playoffs, he made me take them off before coming into the same room as the TV so I wouldn't hex the team. *(Beat.)* After we split up, you'd think I'd have stuck with my Birkenstocks, but no. I started wearing heels again. Oh the pain, I can't think. But I look gorgeous. I had to choose — heels or think. I chose heels.

SCENE 22

Clothesline: I Just Want to Say …

I just want to say, jumpsuits. Can we for one second talk about what a nightmare it is to go to the bathroom in a jumpsuit?

I just want to say that I personally have a rule against sleeveless turtleneck sweaters. I don't understand them. Are you hot or are you cold? Make up your mind.

I just want to say when you start wearing Eileen Fisher you might as well say, "I give up."

NORA. I just want to say …

SCENE 23

I Hate My Purse

NORA. I hate my purse. I absolutely hate it. If you're one of those women who think there's something great about purses, don't even bother listening because I have nothing to say to you. This is for women who hate their purses, who are bad at purses, who understand that their purses are reflections of negligent housekeeping, hopeless disorganization, a chronic inability to throw anything away, and an ongoing failure to handle the obligations of a demanding and difficult accessory — the obligation, for example, that it should in some way match what you're wearing. This is for women whose purses are a morass of loose Tic-Tacs, Advils, lipsticks without tops, little bits of tobacco even though there has been no smoking going on for at least ten years, tampons that have come loose from their wrappings, boarding passes from long-forgotten airplane trips, hotel keys from God-knows-what-hotel, leaky ballpoint pens, Kleenexes that either have or have not been used but there's no way to be sure one way or another. This is for those of you who understand, in short, that your purse is, in some absolutely horrible way, you. *(Beat.)* I realized many years ago that I was no good at purses, and for quite a while, I did without one. When I went out at night, I managed with only a lipstick, a $20 bill and a credit card tucked into my bra. But unfortunately, there were times when I needed to leave the house with more than just the basics. So I bought an overcoat with large pockets. This, I realize, turned my coat into a purse, but it was still better than carrying a purse. Anything is better than carrying a purse. Because here's what happens when you buy a purse: you start pledging yourself to neatness. You start small. You start pledging yourself to neatness. You start vowing that This Time It Will Be Different. You start with a wallet and a few cosmetics. But within seconds, your purse has accumulated the debris of a lifetime. The cosmetics have somehow fallen out of the shiny cosmetic bag, the coins have tumbled from the wallet, the credit cards are somewhere — where? Where are they? There's a half-drunk bottle of water, along with several snacks you saved from an airplane trip just in case you ever found yourself starving and unaccountably craving a piece of cheese that tastes like plastic. Perhaps you can fit your sneakers into your purse. Yes, by God, you can! Before you know it, everything you own is in your purse. You could flee the Cossacks with your purse. But when you open it up, you can't find a thing: your purse is a big dark hole full of stuff that you spend hours fishing around for. What's the solution? I tried spending quite a lot of money on a purse, the theory being that having an expensive purse would inspire me to become a different person, but that didn't work. I also tried one of those Prada backpack purses, but I stuffed so much into it I looked like a sherpa. Then, one day, I found myself in Paris with a friend who announced that her goal for the week was to buy a vintage Kelly bag. I had never heard of a Kelly bag. My friend looked at me as if I had spent the century asleep in a cave. And she explained: a Kelly bag was an Hermes bag first made in the 1950s that Grace Kelly had made famous; hence the name. It was a classic. My friend had heard that there was a dealer in the flea market who had several for sale. How much is this purse going to cost, I asked. I practically expired when she told me: about $6000. Well, we went to the flea market and there was the Kelly bag. I didn't know what to say. It looked like the sort of bag my mother used to carry. It barely held anything and it hung stiffly on my friend's arm. I may not be good at purses, but I know that any purse that hangs over your arm (instead of on your shoulder) immobilizes half your body and more important, adds ten years. Anyway, my friend bought her Kelly bag. It cost only 5600 dollars. The color wasn't exactly what she wanted, but it was in wonderful shape. Of course it would have to be waterproofed immediately because it would lose half its value if it got caught in the rain. Waterproofed? Caught in the rain? It never crossed my mind to worry about a purse being caught in the rain. Thank God it was time for lunch. We all went to a bistro, and the Kelly bag was placed in the center of the table, where it sat like a small shrine to a shopping victory. And then, outside, it began to rain. My friend's eyes began to well with tears. Her lips closed tightly. In fact, to be completely truthful, her lips actually pursed. It was pouring rain and she hadn't had the Kelly bag waterproofed. She would have to sit there all afternoon and wait for the rain to end rather than expose the bag to a droplet of moisture. It crossed my mind that she and her Kelly bag might have to sit there forever. She would get old (although her Kelly bag would not) and eventually she and the bag would, like some modern version of Lot's wife, metamorphose into a monument to what happens to people who care too much about purses. At that point I gave up. I came back to New York and bought myself a purse. Well, it's not a purse exactly. It's a bag. It's definitely the best bag I have ever owned. It's yellow and blue — so it matches nothing at all and therefore, on a deep level, matches everything. It's made of vinyl and is completely waterproof. It is equally unattractive in all seasons of the year. It cost next to nothing ($26) and I will never have to replace it because it seems to be completely indestructible. What's more, never having been in style, it can never go out of style. It doesn't work for everything, I admit: on rare occasions, I'm forced to use a purse, one that I hate. But mostly I go everywhere with my yellow-and-blue vinyl bag. And wherever I go, people say to me, I love that bag. Where did you get that bag? That is the greatest bag. *(Hanging on the back of her chair is a MetroCard bag, which she shows to the audience.)* The MetroCard bag. Buy one.

SCENE 24

Brides

LISA. I never thought I would get married.

AMANDA. I'm not somebody who dreamed of my wedding from a young age. I did not have visions. I just wanted a dress I could twirl around in.

LISA. But two months before my wedding I saw an ad that said, "Wedding Dress Sample Sale." So Saturday at 11 A.M. I was standing with 40 other brides-to-be in front of a store called "Brides 2 Be." They opened the doors and, stampede. Everyone's yelling, "Eights over here," "Twelves over here," "Mom, where are you?" and just grabbing, purses swinging, elbows jabbing, and somehow I ended up with 15 other women in a dressing room with no curtain, stuck inside a wedding dress, and when I finally got a look at myself I thought, *Who is this person?*

AMANDA. I went to all the San Francisco department stores and tried on white bridal dresses with satin tops and big fancy bottoms. It was like going back centuries and the layers felt fantastic, but I don't look good in white. So no white.

LISA. So now I'm thinking pants. Wide, flowing pants, maybe in silk, although I saw this parachute fabric once that was beautiful.

AMANDA. My mom was totally involved.

LISA. My mother and I were barely speaking.

AMANDA. We went to all these boutiques, where the people were just fashion freaks. And they were so excited that I was getting married that we got carried away and bought this dress. It was dark green. Right after, we went to see the rabbi to talk about the wedding and my mother said, "Try it on for Rabbi Mendelson," so I went into the ladies' room at the temple and tried it on. I looked into the mirror, which wasn't easy because it was above the sink — I had to jump up and down — and then it hit me. I looked like a pine tree. I took it off and stuffed it back into the bag and realized, This is going to be hard. This is going to be really hard.

LISA. I've been dealing with my parents' homophobia since I

was a young teenager. I thought they were going to get there, but when I told them I was getting married, they hit the roof. But my fiancée's mother was great. Right after we told her the news, she came right over with an old plastic sandwich bag full of family rings. She said to me, "I want you to pick the ring you want to get married in. Whatever ring you want, I'd like to give it to you." I picked a plain band made of rose gold that was my fiancée's grandmother's. It was made in the 1880s. It's really beautiful and magical.

AMANDA. About this time, my mother went to a Buddhist retreat in Napa.

LISA. Finally my friend suggested we go to a tuxedo store.

AMANDA. She called me up from a dress store in Yountville and she said, "I have found your dress. I have found it, this is it." I'm kind of laughing at my mother and my hopes aren't even up. She says, "I'll be back Sunday."

LISA. I tried on tuxedo pants, and they were slinky and sort of great —

AMANDA. At three o'clock on Sunday, I get a call from my mother, "I am three hours away."

LISA. — and a white frilly shirt that fit perfectly —

AMANDA. "It's me again. I am two hours away."

LISA. And then the saleswoman found a vest with a daisy chain pattern —

AMANDA. "Set your watch. I'm five minutes from the exit."

LISA. Well, not daisies, just the chain part. Interlocking circles.

AMANDA. My mom was like bubbling over with excitement. And she took the dress out of the box. It was the most beautiful color. Eggplanty maroon.

LISA. So okay I did not look like a bride. But I looked … good.

AMANDA. I tried it on and it was amazing. My mother literally starts screaming and running around in circles. She's so excited about the dress, she's so excited that she's the one who found it, she's so excited because I look so beautiful. I just felt completely at peace.

LISA. A few days later, my fiancée's mom came over, and we tried on our outfits and she said, we needed to go together, you know, we needed to match better. So she brought these button covers for the buttons on my vest. Eggplanty maroon. *(She turns to Amanda.)* I, Lisa, take thee Amanda, to be my partner for life, to love, honor, be faithful to through good times and bad, as long as we both shall live.

AMANDA. I, Amanda, take thee Lisa, to be my partner for life, to love, honor, be faithful to through good times and bad, as long as we both shall live.

LISA. My mother kept saying to everyone, "Why'd they have to do this?"

AMANDA. I could hear my mom sniffling, right through the ceremony.

LISA. She even said it to Amanda's mom.

AMANDA. "Why'd they have to do this?" And my mom said, "To honor their relationship."

SCENE 25

Clothesline: Black

Black.

Black.

Black.

Black.

When did we start wearing black?

I can't remember.

I love black.

Sometimes I buy something that isn't black and I put it on and I am so sorry.

I'll take three in black.

I'll take five in black.

Do you have this in black?

Is this black?

Are you sure you don't have this in black?

Could you see if the other store has it in black?

What about the L.A. store? Do they have it in black?

Why do we only look good in black?

I went to a store the other day and a saleswoman showed me a black sweater, and I said, "I can't buy another black sweater."

You bought it, didn't you?

I bought it.

I feel sorry for people who live in places like Phoenix and Dallas because people there wear things that are, like, pink.

What about all those women senators? In their red suits?

And royal blue suits?

Turquoise.

Coral.

Magenta.

What's wrong with them?

Don't they get it?

Can't we just stop pretending that anything is ever going to be the new black?

Black.

Black.

Black.

Black.

Black.

SCENE 26

Gingy's Story: Part 5

Gingy takes a black felt pen and starts to draw on a white poster, following her own instructions. The instructions can be changed depending on what Gingy is wearing.

GINGY. I'm going to teach you to draw yourself. You start by making two rectangles, one on top of the other. There's your dress. Add a collar, or buttons, or a belt, whatever. Add sleeves. If you can't draw hands, put them behind your back. Make an egg for a head. Two lines and you've got a neck like a swan. Can't draw eyes, close them. Make an L for a nose. A W for a mouth. Curly or straight hair. Three lines make legs and whatever for shoes. *(She has drawn a picture of herself and the black dress she's wearing.)* Now this dress I'm wearing has a jacket, and lacy sleeves, and then you want to ink it in. And there you are. *(She hangs up the drawing.)* I love this dress. It's from Eileen Fisher. So there. *(Beat.)* It's black, of course. These days I usually wear black. Black is always chic — and they say it makes fashion choices so much easier, but who are we kidding? There are no fashion choices when you get to a certain age. I have to wear long sleeves because my arms have gone to hell. My neck, oh God, my neck. I wind scarves around it and some days I look like Katharine Hepburn in *On Golden Pond.* I used to show a little cleavage as a fallback, but now my cleavage looks like a peach pit. Someone told me I can have Botox in my peach pit, but there are so many other parts of me that need Botox that my peach pit will just have to get in line. My waist is a faint distant memory. If I find myself in a department store, it's like wandering through the desert. I feel like a forgotten woman. Actually, when I was young, there was a chain of stores called The Forgotten Woman. Now I am that forgotten woman, and the store isn't even in business any more. How ironic is that? *(Beat.)* The clothes I used to be able to wear are in boxes. *(Her granddaughter Allie.)* My granddaughter Allie loves them. She's four years old, and when she comes over, I polish her fingernails and toenails bright red and let her play in the drawer where I keep all the awful colors of lipstick, rouge, and eye shadow that aggressive sales ladies talked me into buying. Then Allie tries on my old clothes, high heels, and hats. I watch her face as she looks in the mirror and sees how beautiful she looks. I wonder if she'll remember any of it when she gets older. I wonder if she'll remember me. My grandmother, she'll say, my grandma was named Gingy, and she wore completely shapeless black things. *(Beat.)* Recently Allie told me her favorite color is pink so I thought maybe I'd try a pink scarf.

SCENE 27

Geralyn's Story

GERALYN. I'd come to the doctor's from work, so I was wearing a business suit and lipstick. I always wore lipstick. Even for my surgery. When my surgery was over, my lipstick was still perfect. The nurses were amazed. "What kind of lipstick is this?" Deep Scarlet by Aveda, I told them. But anyway, when the doctor first told me the news —
DOCTOR. You have advanced-stage invasive ductile carcinoma —
GERALYN. — I looked over at my brother. He had come with me for emotional support. He was wearing this great pair of faded Levis and a V-neck sweater. He was only twenty-two. I thought, I can't die. I can't leave my brother. He still needs me. The woman who had breast cancer told me —
WOMAN. Whenever you go to the hospital, look fabulous. They can be mean to you. They can rob you of your identity. Put on an important piece of jewelry and always look your best.
GERALYN. My mother gave me a white waffle-cotton robe to

wear over my surgical gown. It was short and glamorous, definitely more spa than surgical. On the day that my surgeon came in to undress my mastectomy wound and I was going to see it for the first time, I wore that robe and my Indian candelabra freshwater pearl earrings. *(Beat.)* Before my mastectomy, I had A-minus breasts, so as long as I was going to have reconstruction, I figured, go for it. When the plastic surgeon asked what size breasts I wanted, I said, *"Baywatch."* And then we got into this negotiation because she said "You're too small to have such big breasts, how about a B," and I said "No, a C," and she said, "Okay, a B-plus," and I said, "No, a C," but anyway, the night before my reconstruction, my friend Meredith sent over this beautifully wrapped box, all pretty ribbons and tissue, and I opened it and there was this white lace bra with underwire. I'd never worn a bra with underwire. Until that moment I hadn't thought of my breast as anything but a reconstructed mound. But when I was given this bra, I realized it was going to be a breast in a lace demi-cup push-up bra. The next day, in the operating room, the surgeon came in and said, "I'm going to show you what I'm going to do," and she took off my top and started drawing on me with a Sharpie Magic Marker. She told me where she was going to cut — "here and here and here" — and it was making me nauseous. Lying on that metal table, the smell of the room, the surgeon drawing on my chest. So I focused on that bra. I just thought about that beautiful white lace bra that was waiting for me when it was over. *(Beat.)* I didn't want a nipple on my new breast. The nipples they make are nice, they look completely natural, but I thought, If I have a nipple, every time people look at that breast, they're going to see this awful mastectomy scar, whereas, if I have a tattoo instead of a nipple, they'll see the tattoo and laugh. I don't know what people I was referring to exactly, but nevertheless that was my thinking. So I started phoning these tattoo parlors and telling them what I wanted, and I found this guy who was so excited. His grandmother had had breast cancer and he said, "I have to do this for you." I wanted my tattoo to be a heart with wings. In Spanish, the word for heart is *corazón* and in French it's *coeur,* so a heart symbolizes both love and courage, and I wanted wings to represent all the friends who'd looked after me like angels. *(Beat.)* After my chemo, these two guys made me a really beautiful wig. I didn't want to wear it. Everyone in the office knew I'd lost my hair, they saw it was falling out, so instead I wore baseball caps, backwards. I had a black suede one and a brown velour, but my crushed red velvet was my favorite. My Aunt Honey gave it to me. I saved all my hats and I give them to other women to wear during their chemo. I always ask for them back so I can give them again. I think of them as magic hats. A good luck thing. You know, if you get breast cancer at twenty-seven, no one thinks you're going to live, but I did.

SCENE 28

GINGY. After I finished making all these drawings and writing all the bits and pieces that went with them — which took about a year — I made some copies and put them in big red binders and gave them to my children and to my two best friends. I was so happy, you have no idea. It was the story of my life. My mother was in it, and my grandmother, and my Aunt Babbie. It was as if they were still alive. They were acknowledged. Because when my sister dies, no one but me will know who they were. I was done. I'd managed to say all the things to my children you don't have time to say. I wanted them to know I wasn't always their mother. I was a girl, I had best friends, we did stupid things together. I rode on a bus once with Dora eating dog biscuits so people would look at us. I wanted them to know. Then someone showed the book to a publisher. I thought, who would buy this? It's too personal. But they published it, and it turned out it was personal to other people too … (*Now the other women speak, overlapping, alternating, reminiscing about their clothes and their lives.*)

It was a green plaid coat and I caught it on a piece of barbed wire …

Navy blue wool tights that kept falling down and making this web between my legs …

Matching dresses with my sister for Easter Sunday, bright blue dresses with smocking …

A gold lamé minidress I wore when I snuck into a Sting concert …

Blue jeans that me and my best friend embroidered with peace signs ...

My first cheerleading outfit, that said "Colts" right across the chest —

Black cigarette pants that I wore one romantic night in Paris —

Cotton candy pink silk shoes with bubble gum pink silk roses on the toes.

(As the lights fade to black —) My poodle skirt, my poodle skirt.

End of Play

ILLUSTRATIONS

Title with pink dress
Brownie uniform
Dress coat with leggings and mittens
Tootsie in green dress
Gingy's mother in a fox stole
Black taffeta outfit
Two blue dresses
Gingy's grandmother
Dora in a middy blouse
Satin evening gown
Coral wool jersey dress
Pink satin dress with bouquet
Chinese dinner dress
Yellow wool dress
Floral print pique dress
Maternity dress
Beige wool pants suit
Diane von Furstenberg wrap dress
Blank card for drawing
Gingy's granddaughter Allie